HELPLINE
TEEN ISSUES AND ANSWERS ™

BODY PIERCING AND TATTOOING

MAKING SMART CHOICES

Robert Z. Cohen

ROSEN
PUBLISHING

New York

Published in 2014 by The Rosen Publishing Group, Inc.
29 East 21st Street, New York, NY 10010

First Edition

Library of Congress Cataloging-in-Publication Data

Cohen, Robert Z.
Body piercing and tattooing: making smart choices/Robert Z. Cohen.—First edition.
    pages cm—(Helpline: teen issues and answers)
Includes bibliographical references and index.
ISBN 978-1-4488-9451-2 (library binding)
1. Body piercing—Social aspects. 2. Tattooing—Health aspects. 3. Teenagers—Health and hygiene. I. Title.
GN419.25.C64 2014
391.6'5—dc23

                                 2012048994

Manufactured in the United States of America

CPSIA Compliance Information: Batch #S13YA: For further information, contact Rosen Publishing, New York, New York, at 1-800-237-9932.

CONTENTS

Tattoos are everywhere. Famous singers and television stars have them. Regular people on the street roll up their sleeves to reveal them. Maybe your parents or teachers have a few tattoos hidden away as well. Not so long ago, tattoos and piercings were the badge of someone who was dangerous, someone who lived outside the rules of society. But fashion tastes and trends have changed, and today, tattoos and body piercings have become a mainstream fashion accessory. But tattoos and piercings are different from other fashion items in one very important way: they require that you make permanent, or nearly permanent, changes to your body.

You can change your hat or buy a new pair of shoes, but the tattoo you put on your skin is more difficult to alter. Although tattoos can now be removed using expensive (and sometimes painful) laser surgery, most people live with their tattoos for their entire lives. Piercings involve a less permanent commitment. However, making any kind of physical modification to your body requires serious thought.

There is a lot to learn about tattoos and piercings before you jump into the world of body art. Making smart choices now will save you trouble in the future. Teenagers are sometimes asked to make decisions that will affect their entire lives. Getting a tattoo or body piercing is one of these decisions.

There are many questions that you need to answer before you go ahead with a body

Making smart choices means thinking and planning before you get a tattoo or piercing.

modification. Are you really ready for a tattoo or body piercing? What kind of statement do you want your appearance to make? What is it like to get a tattoo or piercing? Are you prepared for the pain and possible health risks involved? How do you find a good salon? What if your body modification doesn't appeal to you later? Can you get rid of it? Can you change it? Who should you go to for advice?

Obviously, the first place to turn if you are interested in tattooing or piercing should be your parents. In fact, most states and Canadian provinces require that teens have specific written permission from a parent or guardian before a licensed studio can tattoo or pierce them. But many young people simply can't wait to get inked or pierced. They get—or give themselves—tattoos or piercings before they are of legal age. If you are considering this, don't! Doing cheap or homemade body modifications greatly increases one's risk that something will go horribly wrong.

Most people don't stop at getting only one tattoo or piercing. So choosing a good tattoo artist or studio is like choosing a good doctor or dentist: you want to be sure you are receiving quality care from somebody you know and trust. With good information, you can make smart choices.

If you do choose to get inked, you are definitely not alone. Tattoos have been a part of human history and culture for thousands of years. There are many people in the tattoo community and in the health care field who can offer support and advice. You simply need to ask.

Tattoos and Piercings: A Big Commitment

Tattoos and body piercings are a powerful fashion statement. Wearing a tattoo or body piercing says, "Look at me. What do you think?" Before you take the step of turning your body into a visual statement, you need to ask yourself one important question: Who are you, and what are you saying about yourself?

Tattoos and piercings will affect people's first impressions of you for the rest of your life. Like it or not, they will help define your relationship with others. The simple fact is, when people look at us, they make a quick judgment based on our appearance. Will that first impression be positive or negative? Before you use your skin to announce yourself, you should get to know yourself from the inside

BODY MODIFICATION: A POPULAR TREND

Adorning the body with tattoos or piercings has become so widespread in the last twenty-five years that it is no longer considered the mark of a dangerous outcast or rebel in society. Tattoos and piercings are now considered "body art." Fine tattoos and creative piercings have reached the level of high fashion.

But unlike getting a new jacket or unique haircut, a tattoo or piercing marks you for the rest of your life. A tattoo or piercing is a very private agreement you make between you and your skin. What you choose today will be with you forever.

Turn on the television or open a magazine, and you can see tattoos and piercings on your favorite musicians, actors, and top fashion models in advertisements. The fact is, when tattoos and piercings became acceptable, they became like any other fashion accessory. It isn't the cool sunglasses, new sneakers, or amazing tattoo that make people take notice of you. It is you. Tattoos and piercings are a way to broadcast an attitude. But remember: You can take off the hat, you can return the shoes, but body modification is forever.

First, ask yourself why you want to have a tattoo or piercing. Many people simply respond, "Because it looks cool!" Perhaps you admired a tattoo that your friend just got, or you noticed that popular new kid with the nose ring at a party. Perhaps you think a tattoo or piercing will help you stand out as an individual. Maybe you have

Singer-songwriter Christina Perri sports her tattoos at a movie premiere in Los Angeles. Tattoos and piercings have broken free of the taboos of yesterday to become a mainstream fashion option.

something important to say through an image or piercing on your skin. The best reason to get a body mod is that you have carefully weighed all your options and decided that it can help you express yourself to other people.

The worst reason to get a tattoo or piercing is that "everyone else" has one. You are an individual. Whether or not you choose to sport a tattoo or piercing will be a permanent expression of your personal taste. Don't rush out and get a tattoo or piercing because your friends tell you to. Peer pressure can be strong, but when it comes to how you treat your body, you need to make a smart decision, not one arrived at under pressure. When choosing body art, it really is all about you.

Fashion is more than something you can buy—it is an attitude. "Cool" is a state of mind, not just something for sale at a boutique. Remember that it is you—your personality and your inner attitude—that people will find attractive, not your outer body adornment. If you decide that you can best communicate your attitude through a tattoo or piercing, you need to do your research in order to avoid the pitfalls.

Your first tattoo or piercing should never be an impulse buy. Patience pays off when choosing a first body mod. Many people who have tattoos often regret that first tattoo, often gotten at a young age. Many tattoo artists know that first tattoos will eventually be covered up by another tattoo. You may want to impress your first big crush by tattooing his or her name on your forearm, but what is the likelihood the two of you will still be together in ten years? Another reason for patience is more practical: cost. A good tattoo is not likely to be cheap. A cheap piercing is a recipe for disaster. Even if you have to wait until you save up money or are earning more, it is worth it to get exactly the body art you want.

Whatever you do, do not get a homemade tattoo. A lot of people experiment with tattoos using needles and ball-point pen ink, or piercings using sewing needles. A majority of the health problems associated with body art stem from botched attempts by "scratchers" to get around age and licensing laws or the cost of a legitimate tattoo. The body's skin is its outer defense against infection and disease, and perforating the skin with unclean tools in an unsanitary environment is simply stupid. It can cause infection or contamination with a blood-borne disease, leading to hospitalization and perhaps even a visit from the police—not to mention an ugly, amateur tattoo or piercing.

TALK TO YOUR PARENTS

There is no getting around it: you need to talk about getting a first body modification with your parents. Many parents, no doubt, will be dead set against the idea of their child getting tattooed or pierced. But, in fact, it was their generation that made tattoos and piercings acceptable in art and fashion, so you may be surprised at how much they know and how helpful they can be.

It is normal to have disagreements with your parents, but remember that no one wants you to make smart choices more than your parents do. Be sensitive to your

You need parental permission to get tattooed or pierced if you are a minor. Include your parents in your decision to explore body art.

parents' point of view. Getting a body mod is a sign that their child is leaving childhood and entering adulthood. Do your parents a big favor: don't leave them out of the discussion. Maybe they will support you in your choice. Or maybe they will ask you to be patient and call a time-out until you are a bit older.

Getting a tattoo or piercing at a young age is not worth having a big fight with your parents over. It is an adornment, not an obligation. Some teens get tattoos as a way to rebel or declare their independence. Sure, every teen is a bit of a rebel, but you don't have to permanently change your body's appearance to make the point. And one more thing: if you are a minor, you will have to get parental permission in order to get a tattoo or piercing from a licensed tattoo parlor. There is no way around it. It's the law.

TALK TO OTHERS

Don't be afraid to ask for outside opinions. After all, people like to talk about their body art. If possible, find several adults who have tattoos or piercings. Ask them to tell you how they feel about their body art. Have their attitudes

Tattoo Regulations

In most of the United States and Canada, a person under the age of eighteen cannot obtain any form of body modification without written consent from a parent or legal guardian. Local laws vary, so you should call a local tattoo parlor or police department to ask about details in your location. Most states will not allow anyone under the age of sixteen to get a tattoo, and many tattoo artists will refuse to work on anybody under eighteen. You will be asked to show a driver's license or other ID to confirm you are of age. A tattoo parlor or artist that does work on an underage person can face large fines and, in many places, prison terms of up to a year.

In Canada, most provinces allow tattooing at age sixteen with parental consent. After a teen died from a piercing-related infection in the province of Newfoundland in 2006, Canadian authorities have proposed licensing procedures for tattoo parlors to ensure that they meet professional requirements for cleanliness.

These laws don't stop every teen who wants a tattoo. Some teens try to forge letters of consent from their parents or go to less reputable or unlicensed tattoo parlors. Some have a friend tattoo them at home, often using primitive tools in unsanitary conditions that can and do lead to infection. Homemade tattoos look cheap, and experienced tattoo artists consider them a problem because they are the hardest to cover up. No matter how much you may want a tattoo, wait until you can get one legally at a reputable tattoo studio.

changed over time? Are they still happy with their choice? Have there been any negative impacts on their lives because of their tattoos or piercings? In addition, your school guidance counselor and teachers may be able to advise you on what employers, sports coaches, or colleges think about different kinds of body art.

A tattoo or piercing is not something you can keep secret for long, and there is no real point in presenting your first body modification as a surprise. Tell people—especially your parents and family—that you are interested in getting a tattoo or piercing. Don't let your first tattoo parlor experience be the first time you ask for opinions on getting body art.

ANOTHER OPTION: TEMPORARY TATTOOS

With the growing popularity of tattooing, many people who don't want to commit to a permanent inking choose a temporary tattoo. Are you going to a music festival or traveling around Europe for a month? Nobody will ask if that tribal pattern on your shoulder is permanent or not. Temporary tattoos are a great way to see if you feel comfortable with an image or pattern before getting a real tattoo. In fact, many people, including actors, musicians, and office workers, who have permanent tattoos use temporary ones as well. They apply them for occasions when they wish to appear more fully tattooed without the commitment or cost of a real tattoo.

Most commercially available temporary tattoos last about a week before fading and can be applied easily and painlessly. Some well-known tattoo artists specialize in beautiful temporary tattoos done in nontoxic pen ink. Others offer temporary tattoos made with an airbrush that

A groom feeds his bride as she waits for her bridal mehndi to dry. These temporary henna dye tattoos naturally fade away after a few weeks.

applies dyes to the skin without using needles. To the naked eye, these can look exactly like a real tattoo. The most common temporary tattoos are simple paper-transfer tattoos that can be bought in stores.

Henna tattoos, known as mehndi, have a long history in India, the Middle East, and North Africa, where they are often part of wedding rituals. Henna is a plant that is dried and crushed and can be applied as a paste on the skin. Depending on the process, henna dyes the skin in colors ranging from red to brown to black. It lasts from a week to over a month before fading away naturally and without a trace. If you choose this option, be sure to use all-natural henna dyes. Some commercial dyes called black henna use a chemical called para-phenylenediamine (PPD), which can cause severe and painful allergic reactions.

MYTHS and FACTS

MYTH Piercing jewelry will set off airport security metal detectors.

FACT Most body piercing jewelry is made of surgical-grade stainless steel, titanium, or niobium, which are not magnetic and will not show up on metal detectors. If by chance there is detection, it is very easy to explain. For the same reason, a piercing will not prevent a doctor from taking an X-ray: the jewelry will show up on the screen but will not affect the procedure.

MYTH Tattoos and piercings prevent you from becoming a blood or organ donor.

FACT In states that have not yet regulated health and safety procedures for tattoo and piercing studios, hospitals or blood centers require a waiting period—usually a year—and testing before they can safely accept blood donations from someone who was recently tattooed or pierced. Once you are cleared for donation, you can give blood freely. Body art does not prevent you from signing up for organ donor status.

MYTH A tattoo or piercing will change your life.

FACT Don't expect a tattoo or piercing to magically change your social position or relationships. It won't. Body art is part of communicating with others. Choose the design, location, and art wisely.

Think Before You Ink!

Having a successful tattoo experience is all about making smart choices before you go to the studio. If you are not sure that a permanent tattoo is right for you, think about getting a temporary tattoo first. Many tattoo studios provide them. If you are sure you want the real thing, there are a number of important decisions for you to make beforehand.

CHOOSING A GOOD TATTOO STUDIO

How do you choose the studio for your first tattoo? The best way is to shop around, visiting a number of tattoo parlors in your area. If you have friends with tattoos, ask them about their experiences and get their recommendations. If you see someone with a particular tattoo that catches your eye, ask the person where it was done. Also, many studios now have Web sites that show examples of their work and introduce their tattoo artists.

A good tattoo and piercing studio will be clean and tidy. Be sure that all tools are safely sterilized in an autoclave.

There are all kinds of places that offer tattoos and piercings today, so take the time to get familiar with studios in your area before choosing the one you want. On the low end, there are cheap parlors staffed by inexperienced tattoo artists. On the high end, there are by-appointment-only studios where the rich and famous go for their body art.

When you visit a local studio, make sure it is licensed. Note whether the establishment is messy or clean and neat. Are the staff members friendly, easy to talk to, and well informed? Are they pushy, trying to rush you into choosing their services, or do they make you feel relaxed and at home? Always ask to see that they have an autoclave. This special machine uses pressurized steam to sterilize needles and tattoo guns in order to prevent infection by bacteria or blood-borne viruses. If there is no autoclave machine, simply leave. Also ask about other health measures they take. Do all the artists wear rubber surgical gloves while working? Are the needles freshly opened in front of each customer, used only once and then discarded? A good body art studio will not object to your asking these questions or to your taking a look around the tables.

CHOOSING A DESIGN

You need to think carefully about your choice of design for your tattoo. What you put on your skin will have a great influence on how people relate to you in your future. Tattoos are an art, and art makes a statement. What are you trying to say, and to whom do you want to say it? A sleeve tattoo of a screaming demon skull may make a great impression at a hardcore concert, but it may make a very different impression at a job interview. What are you going to tell people about your Spongebob tattoo in ten years? Choosing something meaningful as the design for your tattoo will make living with it easier.

If you have an original idea, make a drawing and carry it around with you for a few weeks. This will give you some

Tattoo artists often decorate their studios with examples of their work, called flash.

time to see if you might want to make any changes to it and to decide if it's exactly the design you want to wear on your skin for the rest of your life.

You can also go with designs offered by the tattoo artists. Most tattoo parlors offer a series of their favorite in-house designs, called flash. You'll see flash photographs on the walls of the tattoo parlor or be given a catalog—known as a flash book—to browse. Take your time looking through it, or borrow a catalog and come back later. Do not rush your decision.

Tattoo artists say the most popular tattoo patterns that people request for their first tattoos are cartoon characters, flowers, Chinese dragons, and hearts with words in a dedication or slogan. Many first tattoos are job-oriented: chefs and kitchen staff, for example, often like to sport creative and funny

Many tattoos are dedicated to lost loved ones or commemorate an important occasion.

tattoos of pigs, chickens, fish, and kitchen tools. Choose a design that is best for you.

Designs using Japanese and Chinese characters are also very popular. However, if you want to get this kind of tattoo, be sure to check the designs and messages ahead of time. A lot of people who do not read these languages and alphabets create tattoos using them. What you think may be a line from a Japanese poem may turn out to be from the label of a package of ramen noodles. It happens more often than you think.

"Tribal tattoos" are the term for the popular abstract tattoos that don't represent anything in particular, but are simply decorative. They usually come in one dark color. Every tattoo studio offers a wide variety of tribal styles. The most common patterns are based on Polynesian, Celtic, or Native American traditional tattoo patterns.

If you want a tattoo of your own design, bring a photograph or drawing of it and include as much detail as you can. The tattoo artist can usually produce whatever you want, but he or she can't read your mind and see the design exactly as you imagine it. You will need to communicate with the artist and guide him or her along. Take your time explaining what you want. Don't be afraid to object if you don't like the first design the artist produces for you. It's all in a day's work for a tattoo artist. One thing you should know is that many tattoo artists do not like being asked to copy somebody else's original tattoo design. If you have a photograph of someone's amazing original tattoo, you should get written permission from the designer before trying to have it copied on you.

TATTOO SIZE AND PLACEMENT

It is wise to keep a first tattoo small, simple, and discreetly located. This will allow you to get used to living with a tattoo and keep potential problems to a minimum. Most first-time tattoos are placed in areas of the body that are easy to cover with clothing, such as the upper

Native Identity and Tattoos

The word "tattoo" comes from the Maori people of New Zealand, who tattooed themselves over their entire bodies with *ta'tau*. Maori warriors were famous for their face tattoos, called *ta moko*, which were done in swirling patterns. When European sailors and whale hunters began to visit the Polynesian islands in the eighteenth century, many asked to be given a ta'tau on their skin as a souvenir. Soon, tattoos were considered the mark of an experienced sailor.

Native Americans also used tattoos, and patterns from the native nations of the Northwest Pacific coast, such as the whale and eagle patterns carved on totem poles, are still popular. Many Native Americans consider their tattoos to be the cultural property of their tribe and may not want outsiders to reproduce them. Teens who want a Native American tattoo to celebrate a Native ancestor should ask their Native American community about its tattoo traditions. (You wouldn't want to get a tattoo that identified you as a member of a different tribe.) Modern Maoris also are very protective of their tattoo patterns. Today's tattoo artists have developed abstract versions of these patterns that appeal to the eye without breaking any rules. Celtic and Norse tribal patterns are also widespread and very striking, and they don't require permissions.

Sailors working in the South Seas learned the Maori technique of tattooing. Retired seamen opened the first tattoo parlors in seaport areas, and soon tattoos became a mark of somebody who was a wanderer or an outcast in society. During World War II, many sailors and soldiers came home with tattoos. Tattoos slowly became something that was not so scary. Today, many people are again asking for these old-style "retro" tattoos.

New Zealand's Maori people wore intricate facial tattoos. Sailors on whaling ships brought the style to the West in the nineteenth century.

arm, shoulder, or ankle. You may wish to leave areas like your back, chest, or forearm clean for now. If you hope to get a bigger or more elaborate tattoo in the future, you don't want to clutter the space where these tattoos are usually placed.

For your first tattoo, it is probably best to avoid a large project like a full forearm "sleeve" or neck tattoo. If you're not happy with the final product, you're stuck with it. Larger tattoos are usually planned with an artist in advance and done in a number of visits over a long period of time. For this kind of tattoo, it's a good idea to wait until you feel extremely committed to a tattooed life. Give yourself time to grow into the tattoo world, and you will likely find yourself much more satisfied with the outcome.

Finally, in no case should you try to copy anybody who has a face tattoo. Many of the simpler face designs derive from prison tattoos.

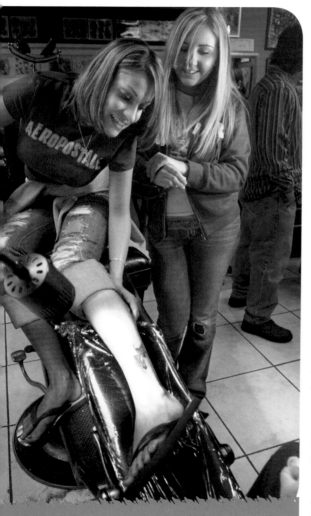

It is a good idea to keep your first tattoo small and discreet.

Prison and gang tattoos can provoke a violent reaction if you have not actually been in a gang or in prison. Avoid them at all costs.

TATTOO PRICING

Tattoos are priced according to different standards. Some studios charge a set rate for tattoos from the shop's flash books and a separate rate for original designs. Many charge a per-inch rate based on how much skin is covered, while others charge by the hour. It is not a very good idea to choose a tattoo parlor based on who offers the cheapest prices. In body art, like everything else, you get what you pay for.

When you have chosen your preferred tattoo parlor, you can negotiate a price. You may be asked to leave a deposit to reserve a place in the schedule. Don't worry: this amount will eventually be included in the full price of the tattoo work. On the day you get your tattoo, bring some extra cash: artists, like taxi drivers, like tips. A usual tip for a small tattoo can be $15 or $20, but if the tattoo artist did a fine job and you would like to return to him or her for more work, a bit more is not uncommon.

Tattooing: Process and Aftercare

A tattoo is made by puncturing the skin with a tattoo needle, a special tool that injects drops of ink into the skin. The skin consists of several layers. The outer layer is the epidermis, which is translucent and regularly wears away and renews itself. The tattoo ink is injected deeper into the second layer of skin, the dermis, where it permanently dyes the skin. The color can be seen through the epidermis.

Because of this, the process of getting a tattoo is like voluntary surgery, and you need to be aware of special precautions before getting a first tattoo. Ask your family medical doctor if you have any pre-existing medical conditions, such as diabetes, hemophilia, or allergies, that may prevent you from safely getting a tattoo.

HOW TATTOOING WORKS

Not surprisingly, much of the process of getting a tattoo works like any medical procedure: your health should be the first concern. The tattoo artist begins by washing his or her hands with a medical soap that kills bacteria that can cause infection. Then the artist dons rubber surgical gloves like any doctor would wear.

The tattoo artist will have already drawn your design onto a tracing stencil made of special thermal paper that can transfer a tracing design onto the skin. First, the skin

A tattoo stencil lets you be sure the final design is right for you and ensures a clean and neat tattoo.

is washed using antibacterial soap. Then it is shaved to remove hair and fuzz using a shaving razor with a fresh new blade. The stencil is applied to the skin using a deodorant stick (usually one that is fragrance-free). After about five minutes the paper is removed, leaving the ink outline of the tattoo on the skin. Once the outline is set, the skin is again washed with antibacterial soap. Now the tattoo artist can begin drawing in the outlines of your tattoo using a tattoo machine.

Once the outlines have been drawn, the tattoo artist concentrates on shading and coloring areas, using the tattoo needle to puncture the skin. After making a line, the artist wipes the skin with a sanitized wipe to clean away any extra ink or blood. A modern tattooing tool, sometimes called a tattoo gun, consists of a needle or series of needles set into a machine that can punch tiny holes into the skin many times a second. Ink is injected into each tiny hole. How smoothly and confidently the artist can handle the tattoo machine is the mark of his or her skill. Drawing clean, fine lines with the tattoo gun takes skill and practice, and the skin on each area of the body has different properties.

A tattoo session can take as little as a half hour for a small tattoo to several hours for a bigger one. During this time, you need to remain seated in the tattoo chair in a sanitary environment. You won't be able to go out for lunch or have a coffee break, so it is wise to have a light meal before you go. People who don't like long sessions in the studio because of pain or discomfort sometimes choose to have their tattoos done in several sessions.

Tattoo artists train for months to achieve clean lines and delicate shading with the automatic tattoo needle gun.

Pain

There's no doubt about it: getting a tattoo hurts! The tattoo needle only goes in about one-sixteenth of an inch deep, but the process does cause pain. Different people react differently to pain for different reasons. Some grin and bear it, while others have a fear of needles and break into tears. The first lines—the dark outlines—are often the most painful, as the needles need to penetrate deeper to create dark, distinct lines. Some people describe the pain as similar to being stung by bees; other compare it to having a sunburn. Certain parts of the body where tattoos are done closer to bone, such as the feet, shins, wrist, or rib cage, are considered particularly painful areas to tattoo. Fleshy or muscular regions of the body are less sensitive.

Tattoo studios are not hospitals. They don't provide pain relievers or anesthetics, and for a good reason. Your reaction to pain tells the tattoo artist if he or she is doing something wrong. You can't take any over-the-counter pain medicines, either. Many common pain medicines, such as ibuprofen and aspirin, cause the blood to thin and slow blood clotting. Don't even think about drinking alcohol—most tattoo studios will not work on an intoxicated person. If the pain becomes too much, just ask for a time-out. If necessary, ask if you can come back later to finish the tattoo in a series of short sessions.

During the tattoo procedure, the artist will talk to you and try to make the process as painless as possible, but there is no escaping a considerable amount of discomfort. It is not a good idea to squirm in response to the pain: it makes it hard for the artist to draw clean lines with the tattoo gun. Sucking on hard candy or chewing gum helps. If the sight of blood disturbs you, don't watch. Pain is just part of the tattoo experience.

Getting a tattoo involves some discomfort. This customer tries to grin and bear it!

Tattoo inks are changing all the time. Modern inks don't fade as quickly as older inks did. Also, inks are being developed that can make later tattoo removal easier. Most tattoo inks have chemical formulas similar to the inks used in printers. The ink is diluted with alcohol or water when injected into the needle. Many of the colors are produced by heavy metals in the formulas, such as lead, mercury, or nickel. Some people may have allergic reactions to such metals. The most common allergic reactions come from the mercury compounds used in red tattoo inks; these can flare up many years after getting the original tattoo. Some inks can cause reactions that produce under-the-skin scarring called granulation as well as keloids—hard scar tissue that grows under the skin. The state of California requires tattoo studios to warn customers of the presence of dangerous chemicals in tattoo inks.

HEALTHY TATS

The real danger during the tattooing process is the risk of bacterial or viral infection through the blood. Tattoo tools come into contact with blood from different people every day. Blood-borne diseases such as HIV (the virus that can lead to AIDS), hepatitis B and C (which attack the liver and can be fatal), tuberculosis, and tetanus can be transmitted through contact with contaminated needles.

People who attempt homemade tattoos—for example, people who are in prison—are at special risk. In a year-long experiment in 2005, the Canadian federal prison system set up tattoo studios in prisons to check the spread of HIV and hepatitis caused by homemade prison tattoos.

Due to the risk of collecting contaminated blood from blood donations, the Canadian and British Red Cross require that people who have recently been tattooed wait six months before they donate blood. The American Red Cross requires a waiting time of six months only if the tattoo was not done at a licensed tattoo studio.

Luckily, there have been no reported cases of HIV transmission by a licensed tattoo parlor in North America yet, thanks to practices such as using autoclaves to sterilize tools. Because of its complex construction, simply steaming or boiling a tattoo gun is not enough to sterilize it. An autoclave works like a pressure cooker, exposing tattoo tools to very high heat and pressure, just as hospitals do to sterilize surgical tools. Before any tool is used for tattooing, it should be sterilized in the autoclave machine and fitted with fresh new needles, which should be opened in front of you to ensure safety.

There is some good news regarding tattoos and your health. Studies have not connected tattoos to any of the causes of skin cancer.

TATTOO AFTERCARE

A fresh tattoo is a fresh wound. Healing can take as little as a week for a small tattoo to as much as several months for larger, more complex tattoos. When you leave the studio, the artist will teach you the basics of tattoo aftercare and will probably give you a booklet with instructions to follow. Take this advice very seriously. You do not want to make any mistakes that will interfere with the healing process. Every tattoo artist has his or her own opinion about tattoo aftercare, so it is worth reading as much as you can to know what to expect.

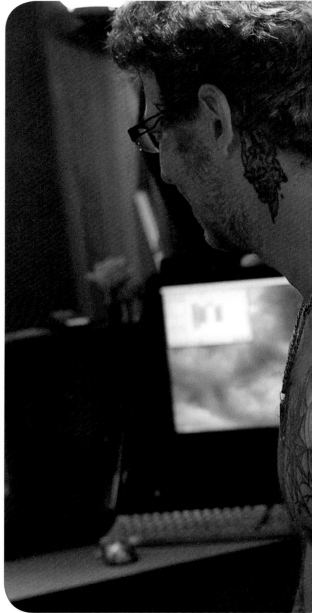

After your tattoo is finished and you have finally seen it in a mirror, the tattoo artist will apply some antibacterial ointment and cover the tattoo with a bandage. The bandage should remain on for at least two, but no more than four, hours after the tattoo process. Avoid the urge to rip off the bandage to show off your new tattoo. Some

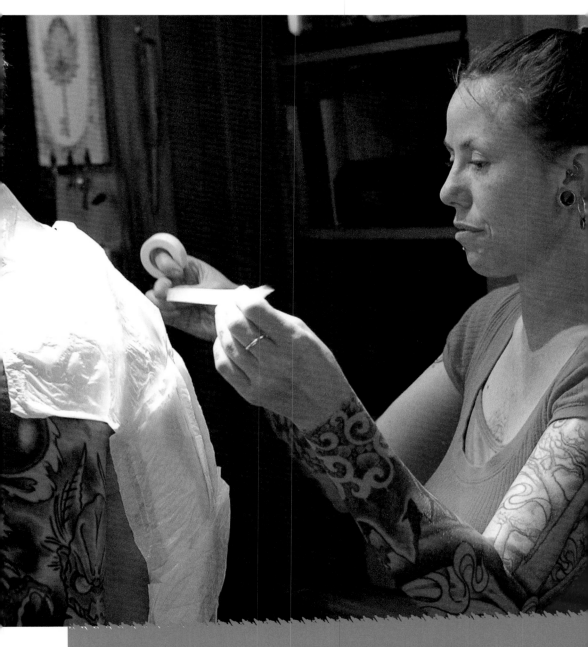

Proper aftercare is the most important part of a healthy healing process. Tattoo aftercare can last for months, but it is worth the effort.

artists wrap the fresh tattoo wound in clear plastic wrap, but this doesn't allow air to flow to the wound and therefore should be avoided. When you do remove the bandage, it may stick to the wound. In this case, just soak the bandage in pure water and wait a few minutes before carefully removing it.

Carefully wash your new tattoo several times a day, patting it dry with a fresh paper towel. At this early stage in the healing, avoid swimming or taking baths. It's fine to take a short shower, but do not soak the tattoo for a long time in water. Tattoo ointments are applied to the area two or three times a day to promote healing and prevent the wound from drying out and building up scabs. The skin needs to stay moist but not wet.

This first stage of healing usually lasts between five days and a week. After this, you will notice the skin on the tattoo begin to redden and peel, like skin with a bad sunburn. You may also feel itchy or irritated and want to scratch or pick bits of dead skin from the tattoo area. Don't! The new skin is very fragile. Scratching or rubbing it can cause scabs to grow, which can break up dark lines and cause inks to run and fade. If areas become inflamed, they can scar and form keloids—hard, bumpy tissue deep beneath the skin. If the itch becomes too bad, lightly slap the tattooed area or spray on some rubbing alcohol. Depending on the size and location of your tattoo, the healing can take several weeks to several months. Do not try shaving the tattooed area until the healing process is completely finished.

Once your tattoo has healed, avoid exposing it to direct sunlight, which can burn the skin and cause inks to fade. If you go to the beach, use a strong sunblock—SPF 30 or greater—or keep the tattooed area covered up. Have you ever seen a greenish, faded smear of a tattoo on someone at the beach? That person didn't use sunblock. Your tattoo will need to be protected from sun damage for as long as you have it. Tattoo studios offer a variety of special creams and lotions designed to keep tattoos from fading.

CHAPTER 4

Body Piercing: What You Need to Know

Body piercing is the practice of making holes (actually, controlled surgical wounds) in the body to place or hang jewelry. Piercing and other forms of body modification, such as scarification—the practice of intentionally creating patterns of scar tissue—are among the oldest and most widespread forms of body adornment known to mankind. Tribal societies throughout the world used many forms of piercing to adorn and identify themselves. When European explorers first met tribal peoples on other continents, they often viewed piercings as a mark of barbarity, proof that they were "savages." Over the past 125 years, the pages of adventure magazines such as *National Geographic* were filled with photographs of the world's indigenous peoples sporting tattoos and piercings. This gave many people the impression that body art was something that marked

Many piercings are inspired by traditions from around the world. These Indian Hindus show their religious devotion with temporary tongue piercings.

MODERN PIERCING

As tattooing began to spread in the 1970s and '80s, it began to lose its shock value. It gradually became an accepted form of body adornment. Some body art enthusiasts began searching for something more radical and shocking than tattoos.

Punk rock fans in the 1970s pioneered piercings using safety pins and other household items for jewelry.

During the 1970s, men began to wear earrings as a statement of high fashion during the disco music era. The first real body piercing studio in North America, the Gauntlet, opened in San Francisco, California, in 1975 to serve the local gay community, but the fashion soon spread to other communities. During the punk rock era of the 1970s, many fans experimented with body piercings, going to concerts wearing safety pins as nose piercings or earrings. With the rise of television music videos, piercing began to reach a new audience and lost its aura of danger.

Today, most tattoo studios offer piercings in safe, sanitary environments by piercers who have been trained to perform the procedures with as little risk as possible. Body piercing is a form of minor surgery and therefore should never be attempted at home or in any place besides the studio of an experienced and professional piercer.

HOW PIERCING WORKS

Many people think of body piercing as a less permanent way of marking your body than tattoos. When you have been pierced, a small wound heals around the metal bar or stud that holds the jewelry, allowing you to remove it for short periods of time if you wish. Removing a piercing, such as an earring, for too long will cause the pieced body part to begin to heal. Depending on the area pierced, a small scar may remain. Some piercings, such as a scalpel cut to allow the earlobe to be stretched to accept an ear plug, have to be surgically

Tribal Piercing

In traditional indigenous cultures, body piercings function as both artistic adornment and as marks of achievement, status, or group identity. Body modification is often part of rites of passage, which mark the change from being a child to being accepted as an adult in a society. The pain accompanying these rituals is intended to be remembered for people's entire lives, along with the cultural lessons of the ceremony. The Aboriginal peoples of Australia traditionally practiced scarification, which involved cutting the skin to produce scars. Among the Yoruba people of Nigeria, it is common for any respectable person to have several small incisions made in the face or cheeks. These scar into a pattern that proudly announces the town or tribal division of the wearer.

Other cultures often hold standards of beauty that are very different from those of our own Western culture. Alaskan Inuit people wore stone or ivory labrets inserted in their cheeks and chin areas. Archaeologists have uncovered ancient labret ornaments that may be among the oldest jewelry known to man. Many Native American peoples wore heavy rings and pendants in their ears, permanently stretching the earlobes to shoulder length. Perhaps the most influential of these traditions in the modern piercing movement were images of people from India and Ceylon who wore jeweled nose piercings, elaborate earrings, and at some religious ceremonies, long metal skewers piercing the cheeks and tongue.

sewn closed if the wearer changes his or her mind. Body piercings require more care and effort to maintain than a tattoo, so think carefully when you choose to get a piercing.

Because everyone's body is different, there is no telling how your body will react to a new piercing. The body's natural reaction to any foreign object is to protect itself from infection and reject any intruding object. This is what happens when your body slowly pushes a wooden splinter out of your foot. The same thing happens with some piercings, depending on the location and type of jewelry used. Some piercings will remain stable with few problems. Others, however, may begin to "migrate" in response to rejection by the body. This is common with surface piercings. With this kind of piercing, a surface bar is inserted into the flesh and the entrance and exit holes appear in the same flat area of skin. These piercings can sometimes be rejected and pushed out to the surface of the skin. These problem piercings must then be removed and the wound allowed to heal.

EAR PIERCING

Ear piercing is the most common and accepted form of piercing. Unlike tattooing and most body piercing, ear piercing is not regulated by law in many places. Many ear piercings are done at home or at jewelry shops, but the best choice is to go to a reputable piercing studio.

The ear has different areas, each with unique properties that determine what kind of piercing it will accept. The fleshy lobe of the ear, the most common piercing site, is soft and has a steady flow of blood, which helps stave off infection. Other parts of the ear, such as the tragus, or rim of the ear, and the rook, or inner part of the ear, are made of cartilage, a denser connective tissue that cannot be stretched and

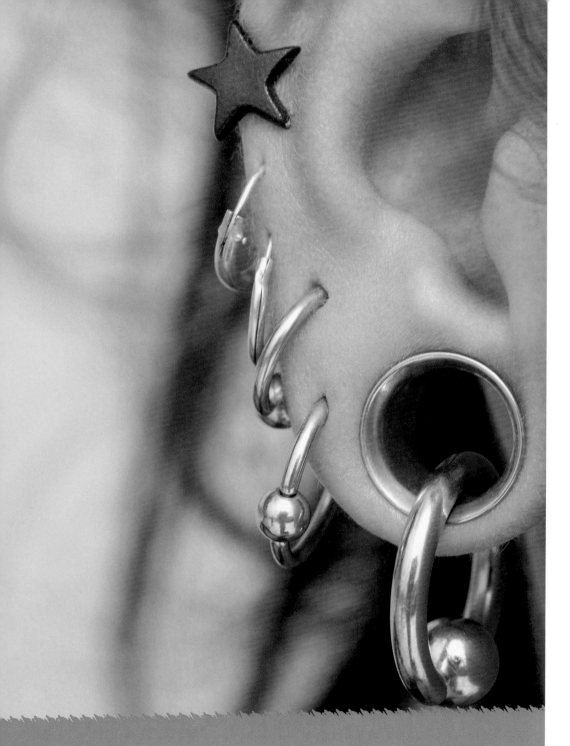

The ear provides some of the simplest—and some of the most difficult—problems for the professional piercer to solve.

requires a much longer healing period. If damaged or infected, cartilage often does not heal back to its original appearance.

Most ear piercings are done using a standard hollow piercing needle that has been sterilized in an autoclave to prevent contamination by bacteria. Ear piercing machines called piercing guns should be avoided. They have plastic parts that make them impossible to sterilize in an autoclave machine. The piercing itself may cause a small amount of pain, but most studios avoid the use of painkilling anesthetics. Instead, many piercers numb the earlobe with an ice cube before the piercing, reducing the discomfort and pain.

Once pierced, a small metal or plastic ear stud is placed into the wound to keep it open while it heals. Studs must be made of a stable material that will not corrode or trigger allergies. Safe piercing jewelry is made of hypoallergenic metals. Many metals used in jewelry are alloys—mixtures of metals—and use nickel, which can trigger skin contact allergies in many people. (If you have ever had a rash from wearing a watch or belt buckle, it was probably an allergic reaction to nickel.) Similarly, gold should not be used for the healing stud: most low-grade gold alloys contain many other metals mixed in. Copper easily corrodes and stains the skin. Titanium alloys or a material called PTFE (polytetraflouro-ethylene, also known by the trademark name Teflon) are the best materials for studs during the healing period.

The fleshy earlobe can also be stretched to accommodate ever-larger ear plugs in the hole. Often, the earlobe is pierced with a surgical knife called a scalpel, which leaves a wide slit in the lobe. The slit is disinfected, and a small plug is inserted while the wound heals. Once healed, larger plugs can be gradually inserted to stretch the earlobe to accept larger ornaments. The earlobe and skin can be stretched to a point of no return, and if made too large, the hole cannot heal back to the size it was before stretching.

OTHER POPULAR PIERCINGS

Nose studs—small bars with button-like tops that pierce the side of the nostril—are the second most popular form of body piercing. Nose rings, such as a captive bead ring pierced through the flesh of the septum, the part that separates the two nostrils, are also popular. Both require careful attention to cleaning because the nose is the first line of defense against many airborne diseases. Infections like the common cold present special difficulties to people with a nose ring.

Flesh piercings include rings through the eyebrow, the lips, or even the skin on the bridge of the nose, called an earl. Piercings through flesh or muscle require special skill, equipment, and aftercare in order to prevent infection. Jewelry used in flesh piercing is much more likely to migrate, or move in response to the body's natural reaction to reject foreign objects. Eyebrow piercings are especially likely to be rejected by the body.

The lips themselves are usually not pierced. Instead, the flesh around the lip is pierced. Lip piercings use captive bead rings or a double-ended labret stud. People sometimes find it strange to get used to eating with lip labrets or studs. People who need to control their facial muscles, such

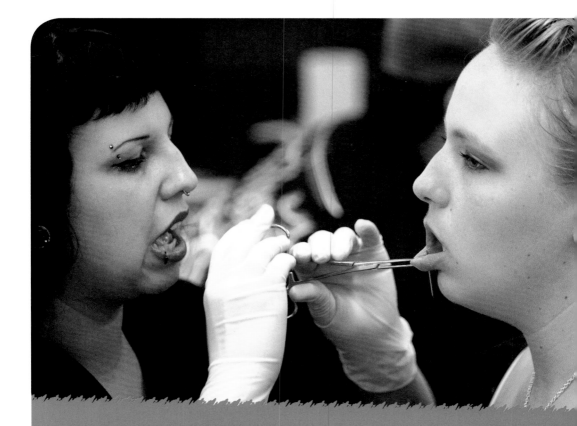

A professional piercer uses forceps to hold a woman's lower lip in place while piercing it.

as musicians who play wind or brass instruments, should not get lip or facial piercings.

Piercings through the face above the lip are called either Monroe (for piercings on the left side of the face, named for Marilyn Monroe's famous mole) or Madonna (for piercings on the right side of the face, named after the singer). Upper lip piercings can be very painful, as there are many nerves located in this area. The rubbing of the jewelry stud inside the mouth can also irritate the gums and cause gums to recede. PTFE plastic studs are best for this type of piercing.

Navel piercings, although common, require a long healing time and special aftercare. Usually, a small stud or ring is used to pierce the side of the navel. The stud—usually a curved metal or plastic "banana barbell"—must remain in place for up to nine months while the wound heals. Because the piercing is so close to vital inner organs, it's very important to prevent infection during the healing period. Navel piercings are not recommended for teens whose bodies are still growing. As the body stretches, the piercings will migrate. If the stud is removed, navel piercings tend to heal with visible scars. Navels, or belly buttons, are not all alike, and some simply cannot be pierced.

Tongue studs are among the most popular piercings. Tongue piercing is a surgical procedure that should never be attempted at home. After washing the mouth with surgical disinfectant, the piercer uses a needle to pierce the tongue. Tongues heal quickly, but it is a very painful process. The initial stud used for the piercing is larger than a normal tongue stud. (During the first days of healing, the tongue will swell to as much as twice its normal size.) Tongue aftercare includes frequent rinses with nonalcoholic mouthwash and salt water soaks to help with healing. Some people suck ice cubes to dull the pain. In addition, people must be careful about what they eat while they get used to the new sensation of wearing a tongue stud.

Tongue studs are also one of the trickiest of piercings to maintain. They can bang against and crack teeth, and if a tongue piercing becomes infected, it can cause a very dangerous infection called an abscess. If your tongue piercing hurts or shows signs of infection (pus, headache, or high fever), see a doctor immediately. Be careful when removing tongue studs; tongues heal very quickly, and the wound can close in even a few hours' time.

EXTREME TECHNIQUES

Modern piercing has developed a number of radical new techniques, pushing the boundaries of body art for shock value. Most of these are not for beginners, and in many cases they can cause permanent disfiguration of the body.

Scarification is done as an alternative to tattooing. The skin and flesh are cut using a surgical scalpel knife in a pattern that will create scar tissue when it heals. Often, these scars are small and are cut into a fleshy part of the body, such as the arm. Larger scars take time to heal just like any bodily wound, and they are easily infected.

Some radical body art fans ask to have their teeth filed into points or have their teeth pulled and special dental implants created to imitate vampire fangs. Another radical body modification is tongue splitting. The tongue is surgically split to resemble a forked lizard tongue. Tongues heal very fast, but the result often causes speech impediments and can only be reversed with expensive and difficult medical surgery.

Radical body modifications like implants and tongue splitting are done by people who make their living in the world of body art: extreme tattoo and piercing artists,

Extreme body modification is usually reserved for professional performers such as Erik "the Lizardman" Sprague. His modifications have included facial implants, full-body tattooing, earlobe stretching, tooth filing, and tongue bifurcation.

musicians, painters, and specialty fashion models. Few regular studios offer such extreme body modifications. Most of the implants must be made to order and are quite expensive. Leave these to the professionals who turn their entire bodies into a showcase for extreme body art.

PIERCING STUDIOS AND YOU

Choosing a good piercing studio is very important. Don't be afraid to visit a few to check out the conditions beforehand. Ask for recommendations from friends or find local studios in the Yellow Pages or on the Internet. Call your local health department to find out if your local area requires piercing studios to be licensed.

The body piercing industry has only recently begun to regulate itself with an eye toward healthy, safe practices. Don't be afraid to ask questions at your studio. Is there an autoclave machine to sterilize all equipment against the threat of infection by bacteria or blood-borne viruses? You can ask if the studio does spore tests to check the cleanliness of its autoclave machine. These records should be available on request in a good studio. Avoid studios that use piercing guns that cannot be sterilized in an autoclave.

Do the piercers wash their hands and wear gloves? Are they communicative and sympathetic to your questions and concerns? Do they discuss the risks and special concerns of each type of piercing with you? If you are under eighteen, you will probably be required to bring in a parent to sign a form allowing the procedure to be done. Most piercers will not agree to perform any extreme or radical piercings on a minor.

Face it: pain is part of the game with body piercings. Unlike tattooing, some piercing can be done under local anesthesia to reduce pain. Most of these are topical creams or sprays that contain lidocaine or that freeze or chill the skin to numb it. Most piercing studios don't use any kind of anesthesia, however, because the initial pain is brief. Avoid taking aspirin or other anti-inflammatory painkillers, since these thin the blood and can cause excessive bleeding. All piercing studios use antibacterial disinfectants to prevent infection.

AFTERCARE

Your piercing studio will give you detailed instructions on how to care for your new piercing throughout the healing process. Careless aftercare is a common cause of piercing problems. Maintaining a good diet and clean habits—just like a patient after an operation—is essential to good healing.

The greatest danger of infection occurs while the piercing is fresh. Avoid touching or fiddling around with your new piercing to avoid contamination from your hands. Dirty hands can introduce bacteria into the fresh wound and cause an infection. Most piercers recommend not removing the piercing jewelry during this period. If the jewelry is removed, bacteria can get into the wound, or the wound may begin to heal and close.

Follow directions for washing the new piercing, and don't use strong soaps, antibacterial creams, or hydrogen peroxide to clean it. These may be too strong for healthy healing. Expect that there will be at least some discharge for the first few weeks of healing. Piercings usually secrete small amounts of pus, forming a crust on the metal jewelry. This is normal and should be washed with liquid soap and a salt water solution. Bruise marks and swelling may be present, especially on navel piercings. If the piercing begins to turn red

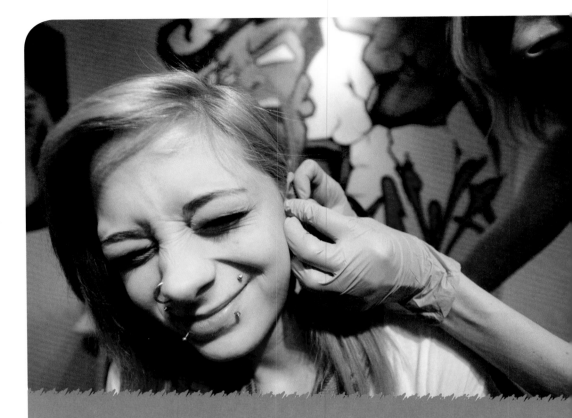

Piercing aftercare can last from as little as a week for an earlobe piercing to almost a year for a navel piercing.

and itch, or if a large pimple or boil appears, or if you feel feverish, call a dermatologist or general physician right away.

Don't rush things: healing may take months. Remember, a good piercing artist will coach you in the specific aftercare procedures for your piercing to make sure you stay healthy. Take this professional advice seriously, and you'll be on the road to a healthy piercing.

10 Great Questions
TO ASK A DOCTOR OR NURSE ABOUT BODY MODIFICATION

1 Are there any skin conditions or health issues that would prevent me from getting a tattoo or piercing?

6 If I don't like my tattoos or piercings when I get older, what can I do?

2 Why is there a minimum age requirement for getting a tattoo or piercing?

7 How can I tell if my body is rejecting a piercing?

3 Can I take a pain reliever or anesthetic while I have a tattoo or piercing done?

8 Can serious diseases be transmitted by tattoo or piercing needles?

4 Can I participate in sports with a piercing or tattoo?

9 Will I have trouble eating if I get a tongue piercing?

5 If I have a piercing, can I just take it out when I'm at school or work?

10 Does an employer have the right to refuse me a job because of tattoos or piercings?

Body Modification and Your Future

Think about your future when deciding to get your first tattoo or piercing. Very few people stop at only one small tattoo or their first earring. Not everyone goes on to get a full-arm sleeve tattoo or a large chest or back tattoo, but if you are committed to doing body art, you need to plan for the future. Do you want your body to be a random collection of different tattoo styles and art, or do you want to work with a dedicated tattoo artist over a period of time to create one masterpiece? Do you want a large, intricate Japanese-style Irezumi tattoo or a striking black-and-gray tribal pattern? You best bet is to discuss these choices with a reputable tattoo artist. Maintaining a good relationship with one respected tattoo artist or studio pays off in the long run. Working with artists who take pride in the work you display on your body ensures that they will help you make

In Japan, tattooing reaches the level of fine art. This work is exhibited at tattoo conventions around the world.

THINK AHEAD TO AVOID FUTURE REGRET

Of course, some people come to regret being tattooed, or they come to dislike a tattoo design that they thought was cool years ago. Many people grow tired of their first tattoo, or they find as they grow and mature that they would prefer to express themselves with a different type of tattoo. In these cases, tattoo artists can design a new tattoo that covers the older one using darker ink. Or they can disguise the old tattoo by working it into a completely new tattoo design.

Inks deteriorate, especially when exposed to strong sunlight. Older and cheaper tattoo inks will fade in as little as a year or two, but modern inks are coming out that maintain color much longer. However, know that after a few years of exposing your tattoo on the beach, you may need a trip to the tattoo studio for a touch-up.

If you have body piercings, you have to be aware of not only infections but also accidents. Getting an earring or eyebrow ring caught while hiking through the forest is a painful reminder that there are times when you should briefly remove jewelry. If you are involved in sports, especially contact sports like basketball or football, piercing may not be a wise choice for you.

TATTOOS, PIERCINGS, AND EMPLOYERS

In some fields, tattoos or piercings are common. Chefs are famous for being heavily tattooed. In other work settings, such as banks or offices, tattoos are usually small or entirely covered up. Unfortunately, there are no laws that prevent employers from refusing somebody a job if they feel their body art is inappropriate for the position. While it is illegal to fire someone for having a tattoo, some companies firmly instruct their managers not to hire workers with visible tattoos. However, as long as you can cover

Tattoo Removal

The most effective method of removing tattoos today uses laser pulse technology. A dermatologist or other specialist in tattoo removal typically does the procedure. The laser is a focused beam of light that penetrates to the dermis—the deeper layer of skin where the tattoo inks are settled. The intense light breaks up the ink into particles that are then naturally flushed out by the body. The laser treatment does cause pain—some say it's worse than the original tattoo process—but the result is clean skin with little or no scarring from the laser. The downside is that laser removal can be very expensive.

Small tattoos can be surgically removed through dermabrasion. In this procedure, a dermatologist "sands" the skin and tattoo off the body. Surgery can also remove a tattoo by excision, or physically cutting the skin away.

A wide variety of tattoo removal creams and lotions are available, but few can entirely remove all traces of a tattoo, and none are as effective as laser or surgical treatments. Cosmetic makeup can cover some tattoos as a temporary measure. This is why you rarely see the tattoos of Hollywood stars in their films.

Tattoo removal—as in this laser procedure—is becoming more widespread as the technology improves, but it is still expensive and painful.

up your tattoo with appropriate work clothes, you will not have a problem in most cases.

The guidelines followed by the U.S. Army and the Canadian Forces offer good advice. Until quite recently,

Body art is now acceptable in all levels of society—within limits. For example, lawyer David Kimelberg covers his tattoos with work shirts at the office. Plan now for a lifetime of living with your body art.

new recruits were not permitted to have tattoos. Today, the regulations state that no tattoo should be visible beyond the area covered by a dress uniform. This means no face, hand, or neck tattoos. Entering a particular career should

not depend on how you look, but the simple truth is that many employers shy away from visible tattoos or facial piercings. The full-sleeve tat and nose rings of a heavy metal guitarist may fit well with employment as a barista in a coffee shop but may prevent someone from finding a good job in a bank or service industry.

THE BODY ART COMMUNITY

If you choose to become tattooed or pierced, you might view yourself as a member of the body art community. There are many people out there like you. The community of body art enthusiasts comes together at conventions held all around the world. Even if you have not yet chosen to experiment with

Tattoo conventions are a great place to start your body art journey. Remember: think before you ink!

tattoos and piercings, conventions are an excellent opportunity to meet some of the professionals in the field, see the latest in flash patterns and body piercing jewelry, and talk to people about how they feel about their ink and piercings.

You may even want to become a body art professional. Tattooists and piercers train by taking courses and practicing their artistic skills on fruit, leather, and paper. An apprentice tattooist usually works as a helper at a tattoo studio, watching and learning for at least a year before being allowed to attempt a tattoo on a person. With the growing popularity of body modification art, there is a good market for skilled tattooists.

Like all fashions, body modification has ups and downs, pros and cons, and fans and detractors. Take time to make a wise decision about your relationship to tattooing, piercing, and other body modification arts. Your future appearance, self-confidence, and enjoyment depend on it.

GLOSSARY

ABSCESS An infected, inflamed pocket of tissue that contains pus.

AFTERCARE The process of caring for a new tattoo or piercing to aid healing and prevent infection.

AIRBRUSH A machine that sprays ink onto the skin for temporary tattoos.

APPRENTICE A person who is learning an art or trade from a skilled master.

AUTOCLAVE A machine that sterilizes surgical and body art tools using hot steam under pressure.

CAPTIVE BEAD RING A circular piece of body jewelry that is enclosed with a bead.

CARTILAGE A dense, connective tissue usually found at the ends of bones at joints and in the harder parts of the ear.

DERMABRASION A cosmetic surgery technique in which the outer layers of skin are removed with a rapidly revolving abrasive tool.

DERMATOLOGIST A doctor who specializes in skin care and skin diseases.

DERMIS The second layer of skin, located under the epidermis.

EARL A piercing through the skin on the bridge of the nose.

FLASH Tattoo designs offered by an artist or studio from a collection of preexisting designs.

HENNA A plant used to make a dye that can be used for temporary tattooing.

KELOID An overgrowth of scar tissue that forms at the site of a skin injury.

LABRET A piercing of the bottom lip, just under the lip line.

LIDOCAINE A medicine used topically on parts of the body to cause numbness or loss of feeling for people having medical or other procedures. It is also used to relieve pain and itching from sunburn, insect bites or stings, poison ivy, and minor cuts and scratches.

ROOK The hard cartilage on the inner rim of the ear.

SCRATCHER A person who performs tattoos, often at home, without proper training.

SEPTUM The thin wall of cartilage and bone that divides the nose into two cavities.

SLEEVE A tattoo that covers the entire forearm.

STENCIL A paper outline that transfers a tattoo design to the skin.

STUD A buttonlike piece of jewelry mounted on a slender post for wearing in a piercing.

TRAGUS The small flap of cartilage in front of the external opening of the ear.

FOR MORE INFORMATION

Alliance of Professional Tattooists (APT)
215 West 18th Street, Suite 210
Kansas City, MO 64108
(816) 979-1300
Web site: http://http://www.safe-tattoos.com
This organization works to inform health and legal offi-
cials on standards in the tattoo industry, sponsors
tattoo trade shows, and publishes the newsletter *Skin
Scribe* to update tattoo professionals on safe procedures. Its Web site offers advice about safe tattooing.

American Academy of Dermatology (AAD)
P.O. Box 4014
Schaumburg, IL 60168
(847) 240-1280
Web site: http://www.aad.org
This professional association of dermatologists offers
information on health issues related to tattooing
and body piercing.

American Academy of Pediatrics (AAP)
141 Northwest Point Boulevard
Elk Grove Village, IL 60007-1098
(800) 433-9016
Web site: http://www.aap.org
The American Academy of Pediatrics provides important health information for teens interested in
getting a tattoo or piercing.

Association of Professional Piercers (APP)
P.O. Box 1287
Lawrence, KS 66044
(785) 841-6060
Web site: http://www.safepiercing.org
The Association of Professional Piercers is dedicated
   to the dissemination of vital health and safety information about body piercing to piercers, health care
   professionals, legislators, and the general public.

Canadian Dermatology Association (CDA)
1385 Bank Street, Suite 425
Ottawa, ON K1H 8N4
Canada
(613) 738-1748
Web Site: http://www.dermatology.ca
Founded in 1925, the CDA exists to advance the science and art of medicine related to the care of the
   skin, hair, and nails; support and advance patient
   care; and provide public education on skin health.

Canadian Laser Aesthetic Surgery Society (CLASS)
2334 Heska Road
Pickering, ON L1V 2P9
Canada
(905) 831-7248
Web Site: http://class.ca
This professional medical association works to

disseminate information and promote quality in all forms of aesthetic laser surgery, including tattoo removal.

National Tattoo Association, Inc.
485 Business Park Lane
Allentown, PA 18109-9120
(610) 433-7261
Web site: http://www.nationaltattooassociation.com
The National Tattoo Association was founded in 1976 to increase awareness of tattooing as a contemporary art form. The association is dedicated to the advance of quality, safety standards, and professionalism in the tattooing community.

WEB SITES

Due to the changing nature of Internet links, Rosen Publishing has developed an online list of Web sites related to the subject of this book. This site is updated regularly. Please use this link to access the list:

http://www.rosenlinks.com/HELP/BPAT

FOR FURTHER READING

Abdoyan, Brenda. *Teach Yourself Henna Tattoo: Making Mehndi Art with Easy-to-Follow Instructions, Patterns, and Projects.* East Petersburg, PA: Design Originals, 2012.

Angel, Elayne. *The Piercing Bible: The Definitive Guide to Safe Body Piercing.* Berkeley, CA: Celestial Arts, 2009.

Bliss, John. *Preening, Painting, and Piercing: Body Art (Culture in Action).* Chicago, IL: Raintree, 2011.

DeMello, Margo. *Encyclopedia of Body Adornment.* Westport, CT: Greenwood Press, 2007.

Gerber, Larry. *Getting Inked: What to Expect When You Get a Tattoo (Tattooing).* New York, NY: Rosen Publishing, 2012.

Hemingson, Vince. *Tattoo Design Directory: The Essential Reference for Body Art.* New York, NY: Chartwell Books, 2009.

Hudson, Karen L. *Living Canvas: Your Total Guide to Tattoos, Piercing, and Body Modification.* Berkeley, CA: Seal Press, 2009.

Irish, Lora S. *Great Book of Tattoo Designs.* East Petersburg, PA: Fox Chapel Publishing, 2007.

Kiesbye, Stefan. *Body Piercing and Tattoos (Social Issues Firsthand).* Detroit, MI: Greenhaven Press, 2009.

Nagle, Jeanne. *Why People Get Tattoos and Other Body Art (Tattooing).* New York, NY: Rosen Publishing, 2012.

Rio, Dale. *Planet Ink: The Art and Studios of the World's Top Tattoo Artists.* Minneapolis, MN: Voyageur Press, 2012.

Roleff, Tamara L. *Body Piercing and Tattoos* (At Issue). Detroit, MI: Greenhaven Press, 2008.

Sanders, Clinton, and D. Angus Vail. *Customizing the Body: The Art and Culture of Tattooing.* Rev. and expanded ed. Philadelphia, PA: Temple University Press, 2008.

Sawyer, Sarah. *Frequently Asked Questions About Body Piercing and Tattooing* (FAQ: Teen Life). New York, NY: Rosen Publishing, 2009.

Sutherland, Adam. *Body Decoration* (On the Radar). Minneapolis, MN: Lerner Publications, 2012.

Thorne, Russ. *Body Piercing: The Body Art Manual: The Essential Reference for Body Art.* New York, NY: Chartwell Books, 2010.

BIBLIOGRAPHY

Association of Professional Piercers. "Aftercare for Minors." 2011. Retrieved July 2, 2012 (http://www .safepiercing.org/piercing/aftercare-for-minors).

Atkinson, Michael. *Tattooed: The Sociogenesis of a Body Art.* Toronto, ON, Canada: University of Toronto Press, 2003.

Atlantic Laser Tattoo Removal. "Military Enlistment Tattoo Policies." 2009. Retrieved July 2, 2012 (http://www.atlantictattooremoval.com/military_ tattoo_policies.html).

British Columbia Body Art Association. "The British Columbia Safe Body Art Practice Act." 2010. Retrieved July 11, 2012 (http://bcbodyartassoc .webs.com/thebcbodyartact.htm).

DeMello, Margo. *Bodies of Inscription: A Cultural History of the Modern Tattoo Community.* Durham, NC: Duke University Press, 2000.

Gilbert, Steve, and Kazuo Oguri. *Tattoo History: An Anthology of Historical Records of Tattooing Throughout the World* (A Source Book). New York, NY: Juno Books, 2000.

Heller, Steven. "Testing a Tattly: Temporary Tattoos Created by Professional Designers." *The Atlantic*, October 13, 2011. Retrieved July 2, 2012 (http://www .theatlantic.com/entertainment/archive/2011/10/ testing-a-tattly-temporary-tattoos-created-by -professional-designers/246262).

Johnson, Kimberly. "Marine Corps to Clarify Tattoo
    Regulations." *Marine Corps Times*, March 16, 2007.
    Retrieved July 12, 2012 (http://www.marinecorpstimes
    .com/news/2007/03/mctattoo070316).

Koenig, Laura M., and Molly Carnes. "Body Piercing:
    Medical Concerns with Cutting-Edge Fashion."
    Journal of General Internal Medicine, June 1999.
    Retrieved July 3, 2012 (http://www.ncbi.nlm.nih.gov/
    pmc/articles/PMC1496593).

Krutak, Lars. "Crest Tattoos of the Tlingit and Haida of
    the Northwest Coast." LarsKrutak.com, 2006.
    Retrieved July 12, 2012 (http://www.larskrutak.com/
    articles/Tlingit_Haida/index.html).

Krutak, Lars. "Tattooing and Piercing Among the Alaskan
    Aleut." LarsKrutak.com, 2006. Retrieved July 12, 2012
    (http://www.larskrutak.com/articles/Aleut/index.html).

Kummer, Corby. "Why Do Chefs, and Especially
    Butchers, Love Tattoos?" *The Atlantic*, June 10, 2011.
    Retrieved June 29, 2012 (http://www.theatlantic.com/
    health/archive/2011/06/why-do-chefs-and-especially
    -butchers-love-tattoos/240276).

Laumann, Anne E., and Amy J. Derick. "Tattoos and
    Body Piercings in the United States: A National Data
    Set." *Journal of the American Academy of
    Dermatology* 55, no. 3 (September 2006): 413–421.
    Retrieved July 4, 2012 (http://www.bxscience.edu/
    ourpages/auto/2010/5/13/44313724/TATTOOS.pdf).

Mayo Clinic. "Piercings: How to Prevent Complications."
MayoClinic.com, March 6, 2012. Retrieved July 20,
2012 (http://www.mayoclinic.com/health/piercings/
SN00049).

Mayo Clinic. "Tattoos: Understand Risks and
Precautions." MayoClinic.com, March 20, 2012.
Retrieved July 12, 2012 (http://www.mayoclinic.com/
health/tattoos-and-piercings/MC00020).

Molidor, John B., and Barbara Parus. *Crazy Good
Interviewing: How Acting a Little Crazy Can Get You
The Job.* Hoboken, NJ: Wiley, 2012.

National Conference of State Legislatures. "Tattoos and
Body Piercings for Minors." NCSL.org, 2012.
Retrieved July 10, 2012 (http://www.ncsl.org/issues
-research/health/tattooing-and-body-piercing.aspx).

New York State Department of Health. "Body Art—
Tattooing and Body Piercing." May 2012. Retrieved
June 22, 2012 (http://www.health.ny.gov/community/
body_art).

O'Connor, Anahad. "Really? The Claim: Tattoos Can
Increase the Risk of Skin Cancer." *New York Times*,
May 4, 2009. Retrieved July 3, 2012 (http://www
.nytimes.com/2009/05/05/health/05real.html?_r=1).

Torgovnik, Kate. "For Some Jews, It Only Sounds Like
'Taboo.'" *New York Times*, July 17, 2008. Retrieved
July 21, 2012 (http://www.nytimes.com/2008/07/17/
fashion/17SKIN.html?pagewanted=all).

INDEX

ABOUT THE AUTHOR

Robert Z. Cohen is a journalist, folklorist, and musician living in Budapest, Hungary, who studied anthropology and linguistics at the university level. When not writing for *Time Out Budapest* magazine, he travels extensively, collecting folk music across eastern Europe and fishing for trout. While researching this book, he talked to dozens of people in Europe about their body modification experiences and visited several tattoo and piercing studios. He still has no tattoos or piercings.

PHOTO CREDITS

Cover © iStockphoto.com/webphotographeer; p. 5 iStockphoto/Thinkstock; p. 9 Paul A. Hebert/Getty Images; pp. 12–13 SW Productions/Photodisc/Getty Images; pp. 16, 62–63 The Washington Post/Getty Images; pp. 20, 57 © AP Images; pp. 22–23 Tom Williams/CQ Roll Call/Getty Images; p. 24 Mark Wilson/Getty Images; p. 27 Hulton Archive/Hulton Royals Collection/Getty Images; p. 28 Wichita Eagle/McClatchy-Tribune/Getty Images; p. 31 © The Orange County Register/ZUMA Press; p. 33 Brandi Simons/Getty Images; pp. 34–35 Adam Berry/Getty Images; pp. 38–39 © Chet Gordon/The Image Works; p. 43 Narinder Nanu/AFP/Getty Images; p. 44 Keystone/Hulton Archive/Getty Images; p. 48 Medioimages/Photodisc/Getty Images; p. 51 David Paul Morris/Getty Images; p. 54 Martin Bureau/AFP/Getty Images; pp. 60, 66–67 Mladen Antonov/AFP/Getty Images; pp. 64–65 Melanie Stetson Freeman/The Christian Science Monitor/Getty Images; pp. 1, 7, 14, 19, 26–27, 30, 34–35, 42, 46, 59, 62–63 background pattern (telephones) © iStockphoto.com/Oksana Pasishnychenko; cover and interior telephone icons © iStockphoto.com/miniature.

Designer: Nicole Russo; Editor: Andrea Sclarow Paskoff; Photo Researcher: Amy Feinberg